HORSE

Jane Gardam

Illustrated by Janet Rawlins

Julia MacRae Books
A division of Franklin Watts

To Susan

Also by Jane Gardam
BRIDGET & WILLIAM
(Blackbird Book)

31693

Text © 1982 Jane Gardam
Illustrations © 1982 Janet Rawlins
All rights reserved
First published in Great Britain 1982 by
Julia MacRae Books
A division of Franklin Watts Ltd
8 Cork Street, London, W1X 2HA
and Franklin Watts Inc
730 Fifth Avenue, New York, 10019

British Library Cataloguing in Publication Data
Gardam, Jane
   Horse.–(Blackbird Books)
   I. Title II. Rawlins, Janet
   823'.914 [J]   PZ7
ISBN 0-86203-066-8 UK edition
ISBN 0-531-04429-7 US edition
Library of Congress Catalog Card No: 81-84517

Phototypeset by Tradespools Limited, Frome, Somerset
Made and printed in Great Britain by
Camelot Press, Southampton

Chapter 1

Susan lived at Sandy Top. It was a farm on the top of the Hartington Hills.

To get to school she could run down the hill to the road and round in a semi-circle to the village square. Or she could run a little way down the hill and branch off down Sandy Back, a zig-zaggy, rosy, brambly lane, very narrow. Or she could climb up behind the farm and run down the steep slope on the other side.

1

If she went the semi-circle way along the road it took half an hour. If she went the zig-zaggy way between the brambles it took nearly half an hour. But if she went the steep harum-scarum way down the slope she was at school in two minutes. If she had been a hawk or a smallish eagle she could have been there in half a minute by diving down the school chimney pot which was directly below her, round like the tops of the heads of the other children running about like marbles in the village square.

But there was another reason why Susan liked going to school down the steep slope. It meant that she could run across a horse.

2

Not round a horse.

Not away from a horse.

Not on the back of a horse.

But across a horse.

The horse was utterly huge. It was a thousand times bigger than Susan and twenty people could sit in its eye. It lay all across the great slope, one foot prettily lifted and its head gently drooped and its tail flowing free. A very pleasant, well-behaved sort of horse, though of course you couldn't actually see what it was as you ran across it, only when you looked back at it from the stile that jumped you into the village square.

Horse was a cut out. A great big drawing that looked as if it had been

cut round with giant's scissors, and it
had shone very white in the green
grass when it had been finished off two
hundred years ago because it had had
six tons of white lime spread over it.

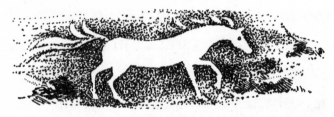

'Horse' he was always called. Not
'The Horse' or 'The White Horse' like
other ones are called in other parts of
England. This horse had nothing
special about him. He wasn't mixed
up with legends or History. Mr.
Grandly at the pub could even
remember his father telling about
when he had been made. Nobody

came fussing to photograph him any more or write boring books about him. He was just a member of the village. Just Horse. And beautiful.

When Susan first went to school her mother took her down the slope as far as Horse's hoof. Soon her mother only took her as far as Horse's middle. Soon again she only took her to Horse's mane, always waiting for her to turn at the stile and wave. At the end of two terms Susan's mother said goodbye from the kitchen and Susan went up and over and down Horse all by herself—though she still found she turned when she got to the stile and waved. This was partly out of habit and partly because it seemed unfriendly to Horse if she didn't.

And she did this for ages—until she was nearly seven.

Then one day in a wet summer Susan turned to wave to Horse as usual but slipped from the stile and fell in the mud. The school teacher, Mrs. Pail, was a fuss-pot about mud, and quite rightly because she not only taught the children, she gave them their dinner and cleaned the school as well. She was a wonderful teacher and Pure Gold was Mrs. Pail, and when

stuffy people said that she *lowered* herself by all this extra work she swept them out of the school on the end of her squeezy mop. She sometimes swept

the children out too when they were muddy, and made them learn their sums in the street on Mr. Grandly's bench. Mr. Grandly kept the door of his pub always wide open in order to miss nothing. He hated children. They needed watching, he said.

So Susan tried to get the mud off. She rubbed at her skirt and her sock and her leg. The rain pattered down

above her head in the leaves of the
rowan tree which had a wire basket
fastened to it for Mr. Grandly's
morning paper to be delivered. Mr.
Grandly was one hundred years old
and he didn't step far afield, not even
to the Shop.

"No wave today then?"
Susan jumped.

Mr. Grandly was tall as a silo,
under the rowan tree sheltering from
the rain. If there was nothing odd

about dear old Horse who was two hundred years old, there was plenty to give you the shivers in Mr. Grandly. He stared far out in front of him with his pale, hundred-year-old eyes. He could see things far away. He could see a hare on a ridge or a sheep in a fence or a lark in the air. They say that the older Mr. Grandly got the further away he could see.

"No wave at Horse today?"

Susan blushed and felt silly. She thought, I won't wave at Horse again.

"About time."

Susan looked up then, cross. "About time what?"

"About time to stop."

"Why?" she said, fierce.

"Why? Because he's scarce there. Scarce there to wave at."

"Susan will you come in this minute," called Mrs. Pail from the school step. "What's two drops of rain to be sheltering under trees?"

Susan ran across the square.

"And whatever's all this mud?" Mrs. Pail tutted and flurried her inside. Susan forgot about Horse then until home time.

But then, climbing back over the stile, she remembered.

Scarce there to wave at.

She looked at the slope above her— it was still raining—and she saw that Horse was not sparkling white in the green grass. Not any more.

10

And he was going all woolly round the edges.

His nose seemed to be buried in a bramble bush. His body seemed to be decorated all over with dandelion clumps. His floaty tail you could hardly see for bilberries and tough black ling. How long has this been going on? she thought. Rain streamed down Horse leaving quite deep channels, spoiling his shape.

Susan thought, It's ages and ages and ages since I really looked at Horse.

Chapter 2

The next day she ran down to school
early and looked in at Mr. Grandly's
open door. He had taken his
newspaper already this morning and
lay stretched out on a very long
wooden sofa in his bar. There was
nothing else in his bar except a huge
fireplace and two or three ancient
chairs on his flat-stoned floor. Several
old photographs of Horse hung above
a table in the corner where the bottles
stood. Horse in the photographs

looked sharp as a horse of glass or steel. He looked pressed out of the grass by a huge pastry cutter. Dazzling white.

Susan looked.

"Get on to school," said Mr. Grandly from behind his newspaper, "I can't do with bairns."

"It was Horse."

"Bairns and attachments."

"I haven't got attachments," said Susan. "What's attachments?"

"What bairns faffs their time on," said Mr. Grandly. "Hoops and kites. It was hoops and kites first. Followed by crashing dolly-carts. Followed by scooters. Followed by bikes, from penny-farthings on. Then it was

13

skates—roller skates and skate boards. For eighty years across this square, I've been warring with bairns and attachments."

"I'm by myself."

"Catapults, arrows, darts."

"I've got none."

"It was hoops and kites to blame for First World War," said Mr. Grandly. "It was roller-skates responsible for Second. Then came the skate boards and so I dare say there's to be Third. Too much pleasure, that's what bairns get."

"I think you're silly," said Susan and Mr. Grandly lowered the paper and showed his terrible pale eyes.

"I want to say about Horse."

14

"What about Horse?"

"It's going away. It's fading out."

Mr. Grandly lifted the paper back up again. "I know that," he said.

Susan went away.

"Have you looked at Horse?" Susan asked her mother. "He's gone all woolly."

"Oh, it's just the rain. It makes the weeds grow."

"No. He's different. He's all moth-eaten looking. You can hardly make him out."

"Well this is a third bad summer."

"Can't we do something about him?"

"Well I dare say we shall," said her mother, "one of these days, likely."

15

"Horse is looking awful," said Susan to Mrs. Pail.

"Go on with your History, Susan."

"But Horse is looking awful. He's fading out. He's all over bilberries and weeds."

"We'll go up there for Nature," said Mrs. Pail, "when it fairs up."

In the Shop Susan said to the Post Lady, "It's so wet Horse is fading out."

The people in the Shop laughed and someone gave Susan a sweet. "You're right old-fashioned," said the Post Lady. "Horse won't fade out. He'll be

there after all of us, as he was here before."

"They say," said Susan to Mr. Grandly putting her head round his door, "that Horse will last us all out."

"Who say?"

"My mother and Mrs. Pail and the Shop."

"They keep their eyes shut," said Mr. Grandly opening his wide so that Susan hurried away.

Then she went to see the wood carver. He was Mr. Grandly's son and he carved beautiful tables and chairs and sent them all over the world. He had made the village quite famous though his customers never actually came into the village because he lived outside it, a mile round towards Susan's side of the hill. The wood carver didn't come in to the village either in case he met his father. He didn't speak to his father. There had been some old quarrel.

Susan decided she would take the long way round home. She called in at the wood carver's shop and sniffed up the lovely smell of wood-shavings.

"Have some ringlets," said young Mr. Grandly who was seventy-five and very jolly, "to hang in your bonny brown hair." He scattered cork-screw curls of wood shavings all over Susan's head.

"Horse is fading out," said Susan.

"Who sez?"

"I've seen. I run on it. Every day. Twice."

"Well I never," said young Mr. Grandly, "you're wearing it out that's what it is, Susan. I dare say it'll pull itself together with winter and a good frost."

"It looks awful."

"That's what your father said."

"Is it then," said the wood carver turning back to smoothing the wing of an angel for a church pew.

Chapter 3

Hardly a fortnight later, on a sunny dry day and the whole school—all thirty of them—tearing about for play-time in the village square, there was a noise like an earthquake coming, or a tank regiment. It went on, louder and louder, nearer and nearer and in to the square burst a huge lorry with a trailer yoked up to its back as long as the village street. The trailer was piled high with gigantic pipes all lashed loosely together with wires. The clatter was frightful.

All the children rushed for cover. Mrs. Pail came to the school door red in the face waving a drying-up cloth.

Mr Grandly appeared in his porch like a large dark statue.

The great lorry came to rest shuddering horribly in the middle of the little square and the driver, high above everybody's head, sat examining a dirty piece of paper in his cab.

"Sandy Top, Grandpa?" he asked.

Mr Grandly turned on his heel and shut his door.

"Sandy Top? Sandy Back?" he asked Mrs. Pail.

21

"What about Sandy Top and Sandy Back?"

"Delivery of drain pipes."

"*Drain* pipes?"

"That's it. Forestry."

"*Forestry*?"

"That's right. Government. Planting trees."

"We don't have trees here," said Mrs. Pail. "They don't grow here saving the odd rowan and the hedge trees and the hawthorns."

"You're going to have," said the man, "thousands of them. Christmas trees."

"Where?"

"Up yonder," said the driver. "Over yon scratty bank. They're starting

22

digging any day. Maybe this week.
I've been rushed over. Ahead with the
drain pipes."

"But what about Horse?" asked
Mrs. Pail.

The driver looked at the broad,
tangly hill-side.

"What horse?" he said.

"They can't. They mustn't. They
won't," cried Susan bursting in on
young Mr. Grandly on her way home.
Today she could not bear to run across
Horse.

23

Young Mr. Grandly put down his adze and looked long and hard at her as she told the tale.

She ran out along the road and nearly got run over by a car.

"Susan, good gracious!" said the driver. It was old Mr Grandly's fly-about grand-daughter who always came over Mondays to see to him. "Whatever's the matter? Here, calm yourself down. Sit still."

"It's Horse. They're going to plant Christmas trees all over Horse."

"They can't do that."

"They can. They can. It's because he's fading out, that's what it is."

She shook off the kind arm of the fly-about grand-daughter and ran on.

"Mother," she shrieked, flying into Sandy Top.

"Yes?" said her mother coming through the back door as if she had been down the slope to the village, which she had.

"They're going to dig up Horse. There's men bringing drain pipes and others bringing diggers, and others bringing thousands of Christmas trees."

"I know," said her mother. "I've just heard. I went down with your father to see what it's all about."

"I shall *die* if they plant trees all over Horse."

"No you won't," said her mother. "No sense in dying. We must do something though. Have your tea and do your homework while we think on."

"I *couldn't* do my homework. Mrs. Pail didn't even *give* us any homework. She's all of a flurry and Mr. Grandly has shut his door."

"Oh dear," said Susan's mother.

"And young Mr. Grandly doesn't care. He justs sits staring and the Shop do nothing but laugh and I haven't even told them. . ."

"What we've a need of is that fly-about grand-daughter."

"She's come. I saw her. But she'll be no good. She doesn't live here any more. Only Mondays and holidays. She doesn't care about Horse. Nobody cares about Horse."

"Sit to your tea and be quiet," said her father, coming in. "You're as crazed as old Grandly. He's saying it'll be the start of another war. Stop fretting. There's great goings on, so settle down."

"What's happened? What goings-on?"

"The forestry. They've tried taking the drain pipes up Sandy Back and they're stuck in the zig-zag."

"Stuck?"

"Aye—the whole contraption.

Stuck in the lane. It'll take armies to shift them. There's truck one side of a bend and drain pipes jack-knifed round the corner."

"Oh wonderful," said Susan, and then, "but oh the diggers! The diggers are coming tomorrow."

"That they're not," said her father. "They'll not get past the drain pipes."

"But they'll come round this way. Round the road and up here to Sandy Top and over. All the diggers. Then the trees."

"That they won't," said Susan's father. "Not over my private land. I tell you Susan, sit to your tea and then go to bed."

Chapter 4

The next day Susan woke with a heavy feeling and wondered why. Then she remembered.

She ate her breakfast early and went to school the long way round. She got to the village and crossed the square without even looking up at Horse, or what there was of him. She couldn't bear to.

Everyone was rather quiet and muttery. Across at the pub Mr. Grandly's door was still shut.

At play-time every one asked Mrs. Pail if they could go and look at the drain pipes stuck in the lane but she said no in case they got loose and came rolling down and squashed them all, causing more nuisance still.

There seemed very little to do in the square except make sandal patterns with the big pool of oil the artic-lorry had left behind on the stones.

Then the fly-about grand-daughter came hurtling from the front door of her arty holiday cottage with the gig lamps, looking very business-like and carrying over her arm a clean shirt. She disappeared in to the pub and there were the usual roaring noises as old Mr. Grandly was seen to. "That's better," she called to everyone, coming out again. "I think we're about ready to start."

A car or two and some people had appeared in the square. Susan's parents were two of the people and the vicar was another and the fly-about grand-daughter greeted them. Then a land-rover drew up with an important farmer from over Thirsk in it, and then the vet and then the doctor and a few more, and they all went in to old Mr. Grandly's.

After a few minutes two more people came round the corner. The Shop's assistant and young Mr. Grandly. The Shop's assistant, who was also known as Silly Betty was sent over to the children and young Mr. Grandly straightened himself up, coughed twice, thrust out his chin and walked over Mr. Grandly's door step. It was the first time for many years.

Silly Betty came over and clapped her hands like a floppy seal and said, "Now then children, I'm looking after you today. In you go!" But nobody went in. They played tig and giggled and pushed each other and ran circles round Silly Betty and one or two (not Susan) even ran up on to Horse.

But after not very long at all Mrs. Pail came sweeping out of the pub and shooed off Silly Betty and said, "All's fixed. Come along now. It's Nature," and took the whole school in a neat crocodile with trowels and forks in a

basket from under her teacher's desk;
and they set to for the whole
afternoon, clearing dandelions,
scratching and digging out bushes
and tussocks and ling and even
precious bilberries.

When they had huge piles of these
they stacked them up in the midst of
Horse and set fire to them.

"But it'll spoil Horse more," said
Susan.

"Rubbish," said Mrs. Pail. "He has

fire in his belly. Like the Bible. And so
have we."

Smoke from the fire of the belly of
Horse rose up to the late summer sky
and people in the far-off trains across
the Wolds looked out of the windows
and said, "Look, they're burning
stubble over on the Hartington Hills.
There was once one of those White
Horses set out over there. I wonder
what happened to it?"

Chapter 5

The children were kept after school.
The parents began to come to join
them in ones and twos as the day drew
on. More and more weeds and bushes
and dandelions were piled on to
Horse. From Horse's tail someone
combed out a poor twisted leathery
fox, dead two winters in a thistle
patch. Slowly the little children grew
tired and got taken home, but the
older ones worked on—with trips for

coke and biscuits to the Shop—until the moon came out. Then they began to get tired too and straggled off. At last even Susan began to get tired and was taken home by her mother up to the top and over, though her father stayed on. As Susan looked down back over the slope under the big September harvest moon she could see her father and Mrs. Pail and the important farmer and the vicar and the vet and the fly-about grand-daughter. Young Mr. Grandly was cutting a new, sweeping curve to Horse's flowing mane. Even Silly Betty was bending and toiling still, and old Mr. Grandly stood stately by the stile.

In the night she woke once and

found the huge clear-cut moon shining in through her window and she thought she heard lorries and shouting.

Oh, they've come, they've come, she thought, they've come to dig Horse up even so.

But she was tired and very achy and she fell asleep again.

She woke to a silent house.

She went downstairs and there were last night's dishes about and chairs all anyhow, which was not her mother's way. "Hello?" she called—but no answer. The clock ticked slowly and loudly and said it was nearly school-time.

"Oh gracious!" she said and

gathered up a piece of bread and ran
like mad up to the top.

But the road at the top was blocked
by three empty lorries with white
insides and white spilling all down
them and on to the ground. For a
minute Susan thought, goodness,
snow! Then—still a bit dozy and
scared because of Mrs. Pail and the
lateness—she careered down the hill
again and round the bottom road,
round the semi-circle, past the wood
carver's where all was silent, past the

Shop where not a murmur and in to the village square.

Children were sitting about. Sitting everywhere—on the pub bench, on the window sills, on the rowan tree and Mrs. Pail with the school bell in her hand but not ringing it was standing out on the stones by the oil puddle— and old Mr. Grandly, magnificent in yesterday's clean shirt and a very ceremonial sort of a hat no one had ever seen before was on his doorstep in front of his open door. And young Mr. Grandly stood beside him.

40

All eyes were on Horse—and so at
once were Susan's.

Horse stood there gleaming and
glittering on the bank side. His hoof
was prettily lifted, his head was
daintily dropped, his mane and his
tail—with not a hint in it of dead
foxes—flowed like silver sea across the
green grass.

A little dark man with a clip board
and papers and a brief-case was
standing in the square looking

worried. "I never was told of this," he said, "I never heard of anything like this."

"It's been there for centuries," said Mrs Pail.

"Come in and see the photographs," said young Mr. Grandly.

"It's not on the maps. Antiquities— ruins and that are marked on the maps."

"Horse is no ruin," said old Mr. Grandly.

"No he's not that," said the little man. "He looks as if he was finished yesterday."

He caught Susan's eye. "What do you say to this then?" he asked. (The

42

girl had a queer look as if she might be thinking about laughing and crying at the same time.) "What do you know about this horse?"

"He's always been there," said Susan, "as long as I can ever remember."

When the man had gone away to write a report and telephone people and ask for the Christmas trees to be sent somewhere else, Mrs. Pail herded them all in towards school and proper writing work. "An essay on fir trees," she said. "How they ought to fit the landscape, how they breed flies and you can't walk in them, how they drop needles and stop things growing more than any Horse, how you never hear a bird sing in them and how they look best cut down and decorated up for Christmas. Just a few ideas," she said, "and then we'll write another story about the lovely trees to be found in hedges and along our roadsides in the Wolds!"

As they went in from the square the three snowy lorries whizzed along the lower road. They were marked DANGER LIME with the name of the chemical firm where the fly-about grand-daughter's husband worked.

"Is it lime as in lime juice?" Susan asked Mr. Grandly, hanging back.

"That it's not."

"Is it like in limestone?"

"That it may be."

"Will Horse mind being limed over?"

"That he won't. Make him clean and sweet. And a good sharp shape."

"There may be some trouble," said the fly-about grand-daughter getting in to her car. "I'm away now, Grandfather. Keep fairly quiet."

"I'm away too," said young Mr. Grandly and shook hands with his father.

Susan and old Mr. Grandly were left alone in the square.

"Lot of fuss and hustle," said the old man.

"Aren't you glad we fussed and hustled?" said Susan.

"Well, I dare say."

"Well there then."

"Bairns has their uses. When their minds is off attachments."

He went very slowly through his old door, leaving it open. "Round the bottom road now tonight," he said, looking back. "We want no frosted feet. We forget all this now. We leave yon Horse to settle."

Susan ran over to school and looked up once more at Horse before she went in.

He sparkled in the sun. He shone. He seemed to dip his head at her.

And Susan waved.